THEY CAN'T TAKE THAT AWAY FROM ME

PHOENIX **POETS**

A SERIES EDITED BY ALAN SHAPIRO

THEY CAN'T TAKE THAT
AWAY FROM ME

GAIL MAZUR

THE UNIVERSITY OF CHICAGO PRESS
Chicago and London

Gail Mazur is the author of three previous books of poems: *Nightfire, The Pose of Happiness,* and *The Common.* She has won fellowships from the National Endowment for the Arts and the Bunting Institute of Radcliffe College, is founder and director of the Blacksmith House Poetry Center, and is on the faculty of Emerson College's Graduate Program in Writing, Literature and Publishing.

The University of Chicago Press, Chicago 60637
The University of Chicago Press, Ltd., London
© 2001 by The University of Chicago
All rights reserved. Published 2001
Printed in the United States of America
10 09 08 07 06 05 04 03 02 01   1 2 3 4 5

ISBN: 0-226-51444-7   (cloth)
ISBN: 0-226-51445-5   (paper)

Library of Congress Cataloging-in-Publication Data

Mazur, Gail.
    They can't take that away from me / Gail Mazur.
        p.   cm. — (Phoenix poets)
    ISBN 0-226-51444-7 (alk. paper) — ISBN 0-226-51445-5 (alk. paper)
        I. Title.   II. Series.

PS3563.A987 T47   2001

811'.54 — dc21   00-029898

♾ The paper used in this publication meets the minimum requirements of the American National Standard for Information Sciences—Permanence of Paper for Printed Library Materials, ANSI Z39.48-1992.

Contents

Acknowledgments

Grateful acknowledgment is made by the author to the following publications in which these poems, some in slightly different versions, first appeared:

Agni Review: "Five Poems Entitled Questions" (vol. 43), "Last Night" (vol. 47), "Insomnia at Daybreak" (vol. 48), "To Giovanni da Pistoia . . ." (vol. 48)
The Alaska Quarterly Review: "Not Crying"
The Atlantic Monthly: "They Can't Take That Away from Me," "Young Apple Tree, December"
The Boston Phoenix: "Shangri-la"
The Colorado Review: "Maybe It's Only the Monotony" (spring 1996), "Right Now" (fall 1994)
Gulf Coast: "Penumbra," "At the Ear, Nose, and Throat Clinic" (twentieth anniversary issue)
The Harvard Review: "The Weskit," "Twenty Lines before Breakfast"
Lingo: "Then"
Ploughshares: "Air Drawing," "Girl in a Library"
Provincetown Arts: "Three Provincetown Mornings," "To Begin This Way"
Salmagundi: "Keep Going," "Wakeful before Tests"
Slate (www.slate.com): "Evening" (© 1995), "Low Tide" (© 1996), "Hypnosis" (© 1997), "Poems" (© 1998). Reprinted with permission. *Slate* is a trademark of Microsoft Corporation.
Tikkun: A Bimonthly Jewish Critique of Politics, Culture, and Society: "Leah's Dream"
TriQuarterly Review: "My Dream after Mother Breaks Her Hip"
Western Humanities Review: "I Wish I Want I Need"

"Keep Going" and "Then" are included in *Extraordinary Tide: New Poetry by American Women,* ed. Susan Aizenberg and Erin Belieu. Columbia University Press, 2000.

The author wishes to thank the Mary Ingraham Bunting Institute of Radcliffe College for time and space and fellowship.

I

Five Poems Entitled "Questions"

Questions

What is my purpose in life
if not to peer into the glazed bowl
of silence and fill it for myself
with words? How shall I do it?
The way a disobedient child sings
to herself to keep out the punishing
night, not knowing that her brother
and sister, hearing the song,
shift in their cots of demons
and are solaced into sleep?

Questions

What is my purpose in life
if not to feed myself
with vegetables and herbs
and climb a step machine to nowhere
and breathe deeply to calm myself
and avoid loud noises
and the simmering noon sun?

Isn't there more,
more even than turning to you,
remembering what drew us together,
wondering what will tear us apart?
Does it matter if I tell
my one story again and then again,
changing only a tracing of light,
a bit of fabric, a piece of
laughter, a closed cafeteria—
if I add a detail almost every day
of my life, what will I have done?
Who will I give my collections to,
who would want to use them?
Don't answer, don't make me
hang my head
in gratitude or shame.

Questions

What is my purpose in life
if not, when there is nothing to say,
to control myself and say nothing?

What could wisdom be if not
a mastery of waiting and listening?
Is it my purpose to become wise?

What is wisdom? Isn't it a pose,
the will refusing realms of confusion?
How would I approach it, unless

I learned to love the absence of speech,
even the implication of language,
so violently I'd remind myself

of a friend who detests the mimes
who gesticulate on Sundays in the park,
and has begun a postcard campaign

to Silence the Silent. She knows
gestures, too, are a part of speech.
Would it have enough meaning for me,

to watch and listen, to touch
the warm fur of animals and the sandy dunes,
to drop handfuls of fine gravel

into the graves of the newly dead,
to learn grief from the mourner's tears
and courage from their squared shoulders

as they return, each one alone
to the limousines? What gives anyone
the daring to adore paradoxical life?

Won't I always yearn for and fear an answer?
Will I someday have the one thing to say
that contradicts and clarifies itself,

and without falseness or sorrow,
without strutting or stumbling,
will I know to say it?

Questions

What is my purpose in life
if not to practice goodness
I know isn't graphed in my genes
the way designs are programmed
in the cells of a butterfly's wing?
How can I pretend
that the modest beauty of self-
lessness is not a false glory?
Why hope altruism is part of me,
set into the elegant machinery
by which form and temperament
are generated? The saints are boring
and fictional, their great acts
accidents of a moment, reactions
to cataclysm. What is goodness?
Haven't I tried long enough,
stepped on my own heart, broken
my hands trying to pry it open?
Haven't I lain awake, my head
aching with the chronic dementia
of the would-be virtuous? Haven't I
settled on my right to be harmless,
nothing better? Didn't I fail
at sacrificing, wasn't the last time
it worked when my son and daughter
still slept in their own messy beds?
Who did they think mothered them,
without rage or tears, with no ideas
of escape? Now they are thrilling
voices on the phone, they're at home

in the world, they have discrete selves,
there are layers to them, they are like
poems. What will I do from sunrise
to midnight now they don't use me,
why should I take on anyone's pain?
How will I live if I won't care
for anything in this world again
more than I care for myself?

Questions

What is my purpose in life
now that it's too late for regret,

now that I've apologized
to the murdered dead and the ones

who went with tubes & needles
on ungiving rubberized beds

and the ones who left glowing,
lovers holding their thin cold hands,

compassionate angels hovering
in the sweetish light of candles,

snow folding itself gently outside
over the dry summer gardens,

soothing the streetlights
and the angular cars, and hydrants?

What can I want now but to be
solitary in a white cell,

with only a mattress and table,
my soul simplifying as Thoreau

advised? I know I'll want one thing
on my wall, a framed poem of Li Po's,

the Chinese characters say the moon
is making him homesick, drunk and lonely,

I'll want 5 things on my table:
a block of woven paper; a brush;

a stone brushrest in the shape
of the 4 sacred mountains;

I'll want to look at a Chinese rock,
small and violent like my soul,

mountainous as the landscape
of Guilin, vertical *jade hairpins;*

and then, a gold and red pagoda,
a ceramic music box—

when I wind a key, it will play
a folk song I've heard only once

on ancient instruments years ago
as I sat on a carved bench

watching huge golden carp
swimming madly in the miniature lake

of a scholar's garden in Suzhou;
it will play in perfect time

for a while until it winds slowly
down, and then the dying song

will pull me mercifully back
to my calm, impenitent room.

II

Maybe It's Only the Monotony

of these long scorching days
but today my daughter
is truly exasperating—
Stop it! I shout—*or I'll*—
and I twist her little pinked arm
slowly,
calibrating my ferocity—

You can't hurt me you can't hurt me!
She's so defiant, glowering,
glaring at me—
but frightened,
her eyes bright with tears—
See, I'm not even crying!

I see. But it's the angel
of extermination
I see, shining
in his black trappings,
and turning ecstatically
toward him, a little Jewish girl
tempts him
to play his game of massacre.

—after Vittorio Sereni

Not Crying

Whatever the intention,
a poem about grief is not grief,
nor the expression or cry of it.
So, if I describe a Jewish cemetery,
the small gray or brown pebbles
on the broad sill of a gravestone
("What does that mean?" my daughter
asks at my father's grave.
"Kilroy was here!"
my stoical mother answers,
embarrassed as she is
by an Old Country tradition
which I explained to her
last time, the pebble that says
"I was here," or "always."
Dry-eyed mother, one moment
irreverent and the next,
sentimentalizing father's
perfections—a far cry
from the litany of complaint
still lingering in my phone's
limbic); or if I should describe
my tears as I stood there
with Kathe, nine years after
his unveiling, that would be
description—not crying.

My young cousin ill
at our aunt's open grave
the next row of stones over,
a chiselled row of names
from my childhood my children
will never know. This is paper,
ink, not a heart breaking
—nor a healing, either.
Something I make,
so when the day is over
there's something here.

Evening

Sometimes she's Confucian—
resolute in privation. . . .

Each day, more immobile,
hip not mending, legs swollen;

still she carries her grief
with a hard steadiness.

Twelve years uncompanioned,
there's no point longing for

what can't return. This morning,
she tells me, she found a robin

hunched in the damp dirt
by the blossoming white azalea.

Still there at noon—
she went out in the yard

with her 4-pronged metal cane—
it appeared to be dying.

Tonight, when she looked again,
the bird had disappeared and

in its place, under the bush,
was a tiny egg—

"Beautiful robin's-egg blue"—
she carried carefully indoors.

"Are you keeping it warm?"
I ask—what am I thinking?—

And she: "Gail, I don't want
a *bird,* I want a blue egg."

I Wish I Want I Need

The black kitten cries at her bowl
meek meek and the gray one glowers
from the windowsill. My hand on the can
to serve them. First day of spring.
Yesterday I drove my little mother for hours
through wet snow. Her eightieth birthday.
What she wanted was that ride with me—
shopping, gossiping, mulling old grievances,
1930, 1958, 1970.
How cruel the world has been to her,
how uncanny she's survived it.
In her bag, a birthday card
from "my Nemesis," signed *Sincerely
with love*—"Why is she doing this to me?"
she demands, "She *hates* me."
                         "Maybe
she loves you" is and isn't what Mother
wants to hear, maybe after sixty years
the connection might as well be love.
Might well be love, I don't say—
I won't spoil her birthday,
my implacable mother.
               In Byfield,
in the snowstorm, we bought things
at an antiques mall, she a miniature
Sunbonnet Baby creamer and saucer—

a bargain!—I, a chrome ice bucket
stamped with penguins, with Bakelite handles.
I wanted it, I had one just like it
at home. Sometimes I think the only thing
I'm sure I want is what I have.

"What do you wish for?" I asked
a friend, I was so curious to know
how he'd formulate a wish, to know
if there *is* a formula. His list
was deliciously simple, my friend
the hedonist: a penthouse with a concierge,
"wonderful food," months in Mexico,
good movies. . . .

                    Last night, you and I
watched "The Way We Were" and I cried—
I always do—for the wanting in it,
and the losing. "It's a great movie,"
I said, to justify my tears. I wish
you were more like me. Streisand and Redford,
so opposite it's emblematic, almost
a cliché. Each wants or needs the other
to change, so the pushy Jewish lefty,
Barbara, should be quiet, accommodating,
and the accommodating, handsome, laid-back
"nice gentile boy" should agree with her
that people *are* their principles.
He thinks people can relax a little,
be happy. If only
                    they could both become
nothing, they can stay together.

All her wishing and wanting and needing
won't make that happen. She marches
against the Nazis, the Blacklist, the bomb,
through the movie decades, and he doesn't
want to be a great unpopular novelist,
so he writes badly for movies,
and later, television.
                    At the end
(it's the early '60s), when they meet again
in front of the Plaza, his look—the blank
Redford quizzicality I've learned
is his whole expressive repertoire—
seems to ask, "Why? Why did I love you?
Why do I still? Why aren't you
like me?"
                    And because the director's
a liberal, Streisand's the wiser one,
more human than Redford—she's leafletting,
to ban the bomb, in the '70s she'll be
Another Mother for Peace—the way
she wriggles her sensual mouth
(a mannerism that's become familiar
in the years since this movie was new)
I know she loves him or at least yearns
for him, still wants him, which is more
piercing, more *selfish*.
                    This morning, my throat
is constricted, my head aches, I'm always
like this, this movie reminds me you don't get
what you want, even if you're not weak,
or mean, or criminal. I wish I didn't
believe that message so utterly. Today

I need to believe something more useful,
more positive.
                    Once, when I was a child,
my mother lied to me. Maybe that day
I was too demanding, more likely I needed
consolation—my schoolmates so lucky,
so confident, so gentile. Either
she meant to reassure me, or—more likely—
to instruct when she said (she couldn't have
believed it, the '40s had happened)
that the meek inherit the earth. That was
lesson one of our course in resignation.
My little mother,
                    little kitten,
be patient, I'm trying, it's for you
I'm opening this can of worms,
for you I'm opening this can of food.

Young Apple Tree, December

What you want for it what you'd want
for a child: that she take hold;
that her roots find home in stony

winter soil; that she take seasons
in stride, seasons that shape and
reshape her; that like a dancer's,

her limbs grow pliant, graceful
and surprising; that she know,
in her branchings, to seek balance;

that she know when to flower, when
to wait for the returns; that she turn
to a giving sun; that she know to share

fruit as it ripens, that what's lost
to her will be replaced; that early
summer afternoons, a full blossoming

tree, she cast lacy shadows; that change
not frighten her, rather change
meet her embrace; that remembering

her small history, she find her place
in an orchard; that she be her own
orchard; that she outlast you;

that she prepare for the hungry world,
the fallen world, the loony world,
something shapely, useful, new, delicious.

—for Florence Ladd

The Weskit

Thirteen rings,
then her thready voice
apologizing:

I'm sorry I took so long to answer,
I had to drag these two big feet
from the kitchen. Well.

I dreamt about you last night —
Don't worry, nothing bad happened to you —
We were together in a cold room,

I was wearing a little weskit,
a wool vest, and I didn't want you
to be cold, so I told you, Put it on,

but you wouldn't — you said
that would make you just like me.
You said, I don't want to be like you! —

After the call, I went into the kitchen
to complain to him, to remind myself
that I only want to be harmless—

but even in *her* dreams I'm rejecting;
to confess I'm afraid
my yearning to be good is only rage

to think well of myself—
like *her* need to give, my mother
who'll stand for hours

at the shaky stove, stirring the pot:
I know you hate soup, but take this,
it's good for you —

and I accept jars afloat with barley
and shove them into the freezer,
resisting the gift I don't want

as if I won't be mothered,
as if I've always been
inconsolable. . . .

I'd been away,
I *hadn't* phoned until morning.
Now, that small purchase of time

seemed heartless—Now,
I felt I should apologize
for *her* dream . . .

Then, as he half-listened, patient
and bored, re-folding the *Times,*
I suddenly saw her dream differently,

as if it were not about my rejecting her
nor about her manipulating me
in the re-telling:

Mother, I thought, you must not want me
to shiver, as you do in the chill
of widowhood.

You reach to cover me
in your dream, but I shout
NO! I don't want it!

I'm afraid to be like you!
I refuse to live in your loneliness,
your bitter spleen!

I stood in the stunned morning light
at our round oak table,
feeling for a moment the remorse

and satiety of one who *is* loved.
I granted my mother her tenderness . . .
But then I thought,

Who is the *author* of this dream?
Must I enter her and
invent her maternal compassion?

or—as I've always feared,
furious with her determinacy—
is she still *in me,*

omniscient mother, mother
with "eyes in the back of her head,"
mother from whom there are no secrets—

not even my fears, not even in sleep;
mother dreaming my dreams for me,
speaking in the old tone

of accusation, tone of sorrow,
of irreducible pain, speaking
my own private night language. . . .

Whatever the significance of the vest,
I could take it, couldn't I—
scratchy, smelling of mothballs,

brown with suffering, premonitory
offering I might be warmed by
if I let go, if I give in.

Narrow, color of dry oak leaves
in late November, tortoiseshell
buttons I see and feel,

why can't I accept it, slip
my arms through each armhole,
tug it across my broad shoulders?

Who else would use it?
Couldn't I pull it from back to front
even though it's tight for me,

even if the buttonholes
don't reach the round buttons—
couldn't I be grateful? Couldn't I wear it?

Penumbra

Mother of my birth, how lonely
it must be in the fierce
aftermath of will,

and how I dither, here
with my vocabulary of refusals
and longing, as if

any word might burn us.
Now I long to comfort you
and be consoled by you,

and you—
nothing softened
but the durable, unendurable

body which betrays us
all, and brings the spirit
down with it.

The burden of our memories—
what was once painful to endure—
to what purpose

should I recall them to us?
Yet they are what we have:
what you said, where

you drove me, our plunge
into the backyard river depths
where Daddy saved me—

Clever mother of my birth,
of oatmeal and x-ray vision,
of moral lessons and the world

as enemy, who waited for me
to love you,
as I couldn't help loving,

when your cracked rages
against me had no source
we could acknowledge—

now I want to tell you,
Don't speak, let me imagine
your sweetness, my soothing

devotion, not that harshness
palpable
as a stone curtain

no caress can reach through,
not to us—not to you
furious in your crank bed,

not to me, alight here
on an orange armchair,
while the television goes on and on,

loud, cacophonous,
a million gaudy circuses,
unfathomable circuitry.

Last Night

Mother, when I left you last night
in the forlorn clutter of your collections,
the May sky turning lavender, the lush magnolias
drinking the antique dusk of Commonwealth Avenue

where seventy years ago, you marched,
a small brave daughter of paranoiacs haunted
by Cossacks, your untried engine fueled,
by the blighted certainties of old Boston—

you wanted, you *loved* the deracinated manners,
the kindly condescensions, the classical
education awaiting your entrance, answers
to a child's roiling questions, child

gallantly rescued by Greek and Latin, by battles,
dates, monuments, by algebras and elegies
and sonnets—mnemonics you'll still invoke
for your trying daughter. . . . Last night,

after I'd finally fallen asleep, I hid again
in your attic, my cheek pressed to a green gown
hanging from a splintered beam. Calmed, soothed
by crushed velvet, safe among moth-eaten sweaters,

puzzles with missing pieces, Chinese Checkers,
my right hand brushed a gilt-edged book,

its binding a pale brown leather; gold lettering
tooled in the cover, *The Book of Questions.*

The Book of Questions—it brought *your* mother back,
her glass-doored cabinet, the brass key she kept hidden
until, on Saturdays, I'd beg her to take *The Book
of Knowledge* down for me. I assumed you'd found *your* key

to America there—to the Public Library, to Latin School,
to college. Grandmother would give magnanimous
permission, then perform the weekly sacrament
of unlocking. I'd turn the old-style pages, I was sure

to be filled with wisdom, or—was there a difference?—
with information. On the green sofa, her *davenport,*
in the dusty St. Paul Street Sabbath morning,
I'd touch the pictures, I'd almost touch the Wonders

of the World. I felt secure that history's riches
had been secured for *me* in the nineteenth century.
Last night, I wanted to see the Sphinx again,
the Taj Mahal, the Nile! Last night, in the warmth

of the past, in our attic, I couldn't open
the buttery cover to that tome of questions.
But what could harm me there? What moral
do I think is in it? What do I know is coming?

Is it that in the unfinished moonlit attic,
there'll be no mortal answers I can use,
only my black infinity of questions? *Mother,
I'm afraid of grief, and I mean to enter it fully.*

My Dream after Mother Breaks Her Hip

She can walk
We're in a grimy park in Guanzhou
by the White Swan Hotel

She's practicing *tai chi*
her indigo pajamas and black slippers
just like the other miniature

old women their smooth gestures
their flexibility and serenity
their healed feet tiny

as kindergarteners
and how fluid she is my smart mother
turning aside now to remind me

Gail
stand up straight the spine
is the Pillar of Heaven

But I'm worried and whiny
flailing in the shadow of a tree,
incapacitated as in life

and she turns back
to her new slow motion
Old men squat murmuring

by their confused caged birds
freed like this each morning
from unlit rooms

I can't dream her power away
I'm caught here
in eternity's shade

where I begin to move
gradually gracelessly
to embrace her

Tree   muse   emptiness
cage   world

They Can't Take That Away from Me

The way the blue car spun tonight
on imperceptible ice—that stop-
time: bare pocked sycamores, the river's
black sheen, the football stadium
empty of Romans, the oblivious sky-
line shining like a festivity—
and, shaken, I could still straighten
the formidable blue invention,
slide the delinquent wheels to a curb;

the way, in South China, the car radio
says, believers crowd closet-like shops
to purchase tiny packets of Bear Bile,
a favorite cure-all, while bears go mad
in their abscessing bodies, in cages
barely their height, hurling themselves,
banging their agonized heads at the bars—
lifetimes of pain only, for the ancient
sake of a fierce "medicinal harvest";

the way a mother stirring sweet batter
in a well-lit kitchen, feels the Pyrex
bowl slip to the floor, and it breaks,
and seeing there'll be no upside-down cake
for dinner, shrieks at her little boy

cowering in the doorway, *Look what*
you made me do! and lunges to smack him,
the way she'd struck yesterday and last week,
though he's still as a stalled truck;

the way I felt last night when she hung up
on me, I knew I had hurt her because her mind
's gone, and I refused for my life
to let mine follow again; the way I held
the dead phone, relieved to be not
listening at last—*the memory of all that,*
no no — relieved, selfish, and empty:
wouldn't I choose if I could not to be human or
any other mammal programmed for cruelty?
No, they can't take that away from me

Hypnosis

5th floor . . . 4th . . . 3rd . . . flickering
lit numbers above an art deco door
in the brain's elevator, a polished
marble cage dropping you smoothly
to the luxurious lobby of Serenitas
Hotel — a '30s spa, a hangout
graced by Garbo and Groucho, grège
carpet, gleaming door sliding open
toward the cabanas, the stucco arches,
a giant fig tree dappling the ceramics,
benevolent waiters posed artfully
by cool palmettos, invented only to
attend you. But you're not relaxing,
not yet. Conflict. Distraction. Close
your eyes now, recline in your webbed
reclining chair, try to imagine
imagining a magnetized barge floating
on the East River, attracting your terrors
like little iron filings zipping
headlong through air to settle on its deck
(But does a barge have a deck? where
exactly do your troubles land?) Oh,
you can let them go, they're bits of metal
dust flying elsewhere, until your eyelids
grow heavy, your chest is heaving
in an optimistic imitation of deep

breathing. But your left arm's cramping;
a dire tautness above your right ear;
your jaw's screwed tight as a dill pickle
jar. You'd better abandon that unseaworthy
scow, envision a soothing warm light
fills your veins instead, floods your limbs,
both your legs unravel, your ankles
angle helplessly toward heaven or hell,
evil exits by the ten toes, a drowsy
something as if something . . . . Now a voice
spells deliverance from your half-head
stabbed by familiars of pain, old noisemakers
of the embroidered white pillowcase,
deliverance from Mass Avenue's repertory
company of sirens, racing racing racing,
you can't silence the one who's clashing
cymbals, who's dropping syllables, who stokes
the day's rages, the one who always co-signs
your black pages — or can you? What on earth
could you be forgetting? What's happening
to your mind's habits? What hope is there
for transformation? What vigil is this
selfish exercise interrupting? What fissure —
what fraying — loosens the fabric of fear,
of perturbation? Where are you going?
or have your arrived? You know,
this is no time for these questions,
your lit feet are fluttering,
you're sinking, diving, plummeting —

At the Ear, Nose, and Throat Clinic

One of those appointments you postpone
until anxiety propels you to the phone,
then have to wait too long for, to take
an inconvenient time . . . Late in the day,
an old man and I watch the minute hand

on the waiting room wall. I've papers
to grade, but he wants someone to talk to,
and his attendant's rude, so he turns
his whiskery face to me: "Y' know, I lived
my whole life in Waltham, worked 40 years

at the watch factory—oh, that city used to be
so beautiful, now it's a mess, those Cubans
and Puerto Ricans, they ruined it."
Coiled in his wheelchair, he's mad
for company, probably scared he's dying,

*

and so am I. I don't remember Watch City
as beautiful the year I was eleven,
when Merle and I rode the Grove Street bus
to Moody Street to shoplift haircurlers
and Pond's Vanishing Cream, nickel items

at the Waltham Woolworth's. It was
an old factory town, wooden triple-deckers,
water rats swimming in the oily river.
Merle and I didn't risk a furtive life
of crime in our well-kempt Auburndale

where we thought we were well-known,
and canoers paddled the same Charles River
past our homes. And I still wonder
what could have vanished when we rubbed
the mystery elixir on our silky cheeks?

*

His cheeks sucked in, this geezer could be
my grandfather forty years ago, so
I ignore his racist overture and agree
Waltham *was* beautiful, as the attendant
takes his Social Security card,

and whistles: "Boy, are you old!"
then mutters something else in Spanish.
The number must be low. . . . "1936—
that was the first year of Social Security!"
the old guy brags. The kid forsakes

our ancient history, flexes his muscles.
He's probably been listening
to insults for an hour in the Elder Van,
he's bored and angry—why should he be
nice? Yet hungry for a distracting

fact or story, I encourage the grandfather,
I want to be treated well myself some day,
when I'll need it even more than I do now. . . .

My little bids for attention, my birds, fragile
fluttering words, desire to be visible and seen. . . .

"FDR was okay, wasn't he?" I'm playing
90, it's what I do to make us both
less lonely, reminisce as if we'd shared
the '30s, as if I'd been there, come
from Sicily or Limerick, a seamstress

earning her hard living one town over.
I always sat this way with Doc, years
after he'd retired, his best treasure
(besides my golden mother) a gold
pocket watch, a handsome Waltham watch—

*

a different time, when the things
a person held or owned weren't many
but were permanent, a part of who you were.
So his elegant watch confused me toward
the idea my little dentist grandfather

had some connection to the company,
as if he'd labored there, a master craftsman,
had been rewarded by a grateful boss.
His bit of luxury, the swirling monogram
on the back (which opened with a click),

IR, for Isaac Rosenberg, timepiece
connected by a chain to a safety pin
at his frayed striped trouser pocket;
another pin secured his Shawmut bankbook,
deposits he'd made decades before

*

that I'd inherit, $214, Shawmut branch
nearby the long-gone Waldorf Cafeteria
where he idled weekday mornings
with his cronies, also reminiscing,
I suppose (although then I didn't think

of it), the Good Old Days before
the motorcar, before their children
moved away. Dexterity and skill gone, too,
from his arthritic hands. He relished
those mornings! The black-and-white

tiled floor, the nearly empty tables,
the Perfection Salad, Welsh rarebit,
the "bloomberry pie." The counterman.
They serve an elegant porridge there,
he told me, gourmet of the ordinary,

State-of-Maine-ah grandfather, my *Mainiac.*
The soon-to-be-widowed wives elsewhere,
polishing mahogany veneer, or playing
bridge, or shopping Coolidge Corner
from butcher to baker in prescient

black dresses. Old men and women
so relieved to be rid of the burden
of one another for a whole morning,
of the tired bickering sentences
of long American marriages, of pain

and disappointment. What memories
they'd had of courtships long since passed on
to grandchildren, and half-false anyway,

like studio photographs, mythic stories
they could live with; now forgotten,

the mistakes they'd been too fearful
or devout to rectify. I miss that
cafeteria, the whole *idea* of cafeterias,
although Doc never took me, just pointed
to it on our Sunday drive, repeating

paeans to gray porridge, something no
description's glow could make me want.
Waltham had them, too, free-fire zones
a kid alone could enter with five cents
for huge iced cookies, black-and-whites,

*

half chocolate, half vanilla, all Crisco
and white sugar, chewed in gluttonous
companionable half-light, wonderful—
But who'd know that now? Who cares?
Merle and I did everything subversive

we could imagine—which wasn't much.
I'm sure I cruised Sin City in my mind,
decayed old town—nowhere—but to me
forbidden fruit: the 5 & 10, eyelash
curlers, odd metal torture instruments

I smuggled home that pinched my lids
and made my lashes angle wildly up,
delinquent startled in the bathroom
mirror; Tangee lipsticks the size
of my little finger, unflattering coral;

pink girdles I'd eye furtively, wondering
that I'd have to wriggle into one someday,
or wear the bony corset my grandmother
assured me was my fate. Oh, esoteric glamorous
puzzle of the vanished vanishing cream . . .

*

Later, not *so* much later, the first day
of my driver's license, I drove the family
station wagon down Moody Street and banged
the traffic policeman's rubber perch.
He jumped down before it bounced the street,

and yelled me over in a rage. Or maybe,
he was kindly, it's only my criminal terror
I remember, of punishment fine-tuned,
my ruined life, my new rights vanishing.
Hardly a threat, I know now, the feckless cop.

I gripped the steering wheel so hard
to stop the huge recalcitrant Ford, doomed
to lose my brand-new temporary license—
How could I think, my budding power stripped,
I'd ever get the chance to live or drive?

Girl in a Library

" . . . But my mind, gone out in tenderness,
Shrinks from its object . . . "
—Randall Jarrell

I want to find my way back to her,
to help her, to grab her hand, pull her
up from the wooden floor of the stacks
where she's reading accounts of the hatchet
murders of Lizzie Borden's harsh parents
as if she could learn something about
life if she knew all the cuts and slashes;

her essay on Wordsworth or Keats
only a knot in her belly, a faint pressure
at her temples. She's pale, it's five years
before the first migraine, but the dreamy
flush has already drained from her face.
I want to lead her out of the library,
to sit with her on a bench under a still

living elm tree, be *one who understands,*
but even today I don't understand,
I want to shake her and want to assure her,
to hold her—but love's not safe for her,
although she craves what she knows
of it, love's a snare, a closed door,
a dank cell. Maybe she should just leave

the campus, take a train to Fall River,
inspect Lizzie's room, the rigid corsets
and buttoned shoes, the horsehair sofas,
the kitchen's rank stew. Hell. Bleak
loyal judgmental journals of a next-door
neighbor—not a friend, Lizzie had no friend.
If only she could follow one trajectory

of thought, a plan, invent a journey
out of this place, a vocation—
but without me to guide her, where
would she go? And what did I ever offer,
what stiffening of spine? What goal?
Rather, stiffening of soul, her soul
cocooned in the library's trivia.

Soul circling its lessons. What can I say
before she walks like a ghost in white lace
carrying her bouquet of stephanotis,
her father beaming innocently at her side,
a boy waiting, trembling, to shape her?
He's innocent, too, we are all innocent,
even Lizzie Borden who surely did take

the axe. It was so hot that summer morning.
The hard-hearted stepmother, heavy hand
of the father. There was another daughter
they favored, and Lizzie, stewing at home,
heavy smell of mutton in the pores
of history. But this girl, her story's
still a mystery—I tell myself she's a quick

study, a survivor. There's still time.
Soon she'll close the bloody book,
slink past the lit carrels, through
the library's heavy door to the world.
Is it too late to try to touch her,
kneel beside her on the dusty floor
where we're avoiding her assignment?

Twenty Lines before Breakfast

Is it hereditary, this maundering every morning
like a hermit, hesitating by the solarium
as if a choice of Grape-nuts or dry bagel
would foredoom you? Foredoom to what,

what hemidemisemiquavers are trilling
up there in the brain's gray atmosphere?
What melodious message from which ancestor?
(The blacksmith? The artificial flowermaker?)

Who's watching? Who's calculating your chances
if you choose a pinkish prawn in scrumptious
marzipan? Who's waiting impatiently back there
in the family tree for your marconi-gram?

Who's still got the wireless tapped into
which hemisphere, who's signalling warnings,
who's prophesying, *Come the millennium. . . .?*
What millenarian minutiae ring in your noggin,

what mildewed notions? What thorny hairtree
are relatives waving flags from? Who's decoding
solicitous semaphores flashing in the branches:
Don't go crazy, kid, it's real expensive there. . . .

Wakeful before Tests
Massachusetts General Hospital

Semesters of squandered time. Missed lectures,
stubborn childlike wandering from the subject—
is this what my body's re-living?
The self-inflicted panic of my truant years,
exhilarated horrors of eleventh hours?
Immaculate textbook pages, my clever manic notes
fractured on the unmade dormitory bed—
too late for brooding on what I should have done,
should have read, I'd make do with what I had.
Then—euphoric—I *had* nine lives!
My friends, stupefied by my survivals,
devotees of my antics, where are you now?
Could your laughter calm me?
Did it then? Girls,
this time I'm obeying instructions.
My wakeful educable body
has learned its lesson.

*

No, that's not right. Not obeying,
more, *It's too late, there's nothing I can do.*
In college, I craved extinction—
wasn't that what failure was?—
although like a magician
wrenching rabbits from a shabby stovepipe hat,

or seeming to,
I'd torch bluebooks with last-minute erudition;
I'd pass.

*

Now, behind closed lids, listening to night's
doomy sirens, I see my mother-in-law,
three months before her end:
great scared mascaraed eyes,
her perfumed negligé, the gilt rococo bed,
the champagne cashmere throw;
her friends, all *maquillage,* all mink
and dread, bending their lifted faces
to catch her clubby whisper: *Girls,*
I'm dead.

*

Of course—I'd have to think of her.
I'm haunted by her kind of terrifying
purposelessness, life looking for its mirror,
insatiable ruined desires for reassurance.

She became my education, fathomless, immaterial,
unfinished. Now, tomorrow's a hard table
I'll study on, infiltrated, pierced,
leaning into pain as into a mother's arms. . . .

*

Unfinished work, what is it?
Anonymous headlights, through-line
flashing on childhood's bedroom walls,

images I never controlled or invented,
narrating from bedroom to bedroom:
a wakeful girl afraid of the door

that opens, a young mother breathing
to her children's breath, children
another dream, another promise. . . .

*

The work.
Postponed again.
Tomorrow, a silence,
or a buzzing hive I'll enter
willingly, to belong or
else brave the smart
of its attack, to face or
lose myself in action, to do
the task I thought I came for
as I'm stung toward death.

Shangri-la

Tonight in my father's vanished house,
in the dusty upstairs hall
of my father's house that burned,

a German shepherd lies dying
in the smoky hallway, he's starving,
I know I've left him to starve though

I don't know why, so I rush to atone,
to bring him a saucer of what I have—
of cinders—though this dog who's mine,

whom I've never seen, doesn't move,
his dark heavy head won't lift
from the pine floor to the sooty bowl;

uncomplaining, unaccusing, a sorrowful
monumental dying of which I am author,
more insupportable, more wracking

than anyone I've hurt before
or abandoned; and now there's no shield
between me and anguish when I wake

to the oblivious Pacific sun;
nothing will absolve me,
my loyal dog stays with me,

the royal palm trees sway outside
the window of the Shangri-la Hotel—
day I'd have known had I not found him

Two Bedrooms

Nights I return to this room, to the faded
scarves and sachets, the rococo bed,

its pale percale sheets, the velvet chaise,
the mirrored vanity, stale exhalations

of face powder and Patou, fragrance
of the elevator, opening into 6B—

of you, operatic, negligéed, perfumed.
Here where you died, I hunt for the

thing not here, not in the faux marble
fireplace, not in the gilt frames, not

in the French night tables, nowhere
in drawers of satins and laces. Not

a hairpin or ashtray, nothing from
your collections of eyeglass cases,

lipstick cases, antidepressants. Yes,
I'm still searching for a thing to keep,

rifling your musky closets for what I'd want,
glamor you'd let go of now, let me have.

                        (H. M., 1988)

                    *

I hold to the banister,
                              picking my way
up the carpeted steps,
                              on an errand,
a rescue mission,
                              to find some "purloined"
item:
        a single jet earring, a Rose O'Neill
kewpie,
              one bronzed Shakespeare bookend —
little loose ends
              of a drama
                              that's beginning
to be forgotten. . . .
                              I know these steps,
I could climb them
                              blindfolded, barefoot,
I should know
              where they're leading:
here's my locked room,
                              the twin spool beds
I shared with a sister,
                              covered now
with Buffalo pottery
                              and cartons of china.
I walk in sleep to their
                              bedroom door
where I saw my father
                              square his gallant shoulders
one last time, take
              one last look,
before he went down
                              for good. Here

are the bookshelves
                                of inventory, here
the ephemera,
                                postcard of presidents,
of town greens,
                                of Hitler. Here,
on the night table,
                                a crystal chimera
I handle carefully.
                                Like a safecracker
I feel each "ding"
                                with trained fingertips.
I caress while I can
                                the chipped dusty goat body,
the cracked lion head.
                                But still I don't get
what it is I came for.
                                I turn and turn
back to the stairs,
                                go down empty-handed.

                                (M. B., 1999)

IV

Poems

I still write them.
I imagine them lying
to anxious friends wishing me
happiness at the end of my years.
I write in the dark, always
in a state of refusal, as if
I were paying a disagreeable debt,
a debt many years old.
No, there's no more pleasure
in this exercise. People tease me:
You thought you were making Art,
you wrote for Art's sake!
That's not it, I wanted something else.
You tell me if it was something more,
or less: I think one writes
to shake off an unbearable weight,
to pass it on to whoever comes after.
But there was always too much weight;
the poems aren't strong enough
if even I can't remember a line
by the next day.

—*after Vittorio Sereni*

Michelangelo: To Giovanni da Pistoia When the Author Was Painting the Vault of the Sistine Chapel

—1509

I've already grown a goiter from this torture,
hunched up here like a cat in Lombardy
(or anywhere else where the stagnant water's poison).
My stomach's squashed under my chin, my beard's
pointing at heaven, my brain's crushed in a casket,
my breast twists like a harpy's. My brush,
above me all the time, dribbles paint
so my face makes a fine floor for droppings!

My haunches are grinding into my guts,
my poor ass strains to work as a counterweight,
every gesture I make is blind and aimless.
My skin hangs loose below me, my spine's
all knotted from folding over itself.
I'm bent taut as a Syrian bow.

Because I'm stuck like this, my thoughts
are crazy, perfidious tripe:
anyone shoots badly through a crooked blowpipe.

My painting is dead.
Defend it for me, Giovanni, protect my honor.
I am not in the right place—I am not a painter.

v

Air Drawing

What would be strange
in someone else's bed, familiar
here as the body's jolt
at the edge of sleep—body
persistent, solitary, precarious.

I watch his right hand float
in our bedroom's midnight,
inscribe forms by instinct on the air,
arterial, calligraphic
figures I'm too literal to follow.

I close my book quietly,
leave a woman detective to tough
her own way out of trouble—
local color of Chicago, Sears Tower,
bloodied knuckles, corpses.

I turn to him—
who else would I turn to?—
but I can only watch
for a few minutes at a time
the mysterious art of his sleep.

If I touch his hand, he won't know it,
and it's always comforted me

to feel the vibration,
the singular humming in him,
nocturnal humming . . .

My mystery falls to the floor,
nothing I'll think about tomorrow—
I'm listening for the breath
after this breath,
for each small exhalation . . .

Is this the way it has to be—
one of us always vigilant,
watching over the unconscious
other, the quick elusory
tracings on the night's space?

That night two years ago
in the hospital, tubes
in his pale right hand,
in his thigh, I asked myself,
Does he love me?

and if he does,
how could he let that steely man
in green scrubs snake his way
nearer to his heart
than I've ever gone?

Leah's Dream

". . . for she said, Surely the Lord
hath looked upon my affliction;
now therefore my husband will love me."
—Genesis 29:32

"Then finally I asked you to marry me,
my husband, and we embraced
as we never have, neither of us

breaking away from the other,
our bodies clinging,
breast to breast, sex to sex;

my arms around you, your hard hands
on my back, my face at your neck.
And you didn't break away.

When I said to you, 'I don't want
to be alone anymore,' I spoke
with the passion of an abstinent,

an ascetic hungry at last
for the world's meat and drink.
You didn't reply, you didn't pull away.

. . . Then I woke, it was still dark,
you were sleeping beside me,
snoring lightly, a small tentative sound,

like the teakettle's gentle whistle
when water begins to boil. . . . "

Then

We weren't waiting for anything to happen.
We lived by a lake, no tides to nag us,
no relentless conventions of flow

and ebb. No frantic hermit crabs
dragging sideways in their stolen shells,
nor the drained tidal pools they fled—

only the soft green surround of pine
and beech, the mackerel clouds, the meek
canoes. We felt enclosed. Safe.

The future looked fictional then,
though I never doubted a lucky life
could break, that rapture and grief

could be handed to me in one hard package,
delivered, and left, however I labored,
whether I rested, or ranted and zigzagged

from morning to evening. I worked
with my back to our life. Moonflowers
bloomed in the nightyard: white,

dazzling, sufficient to the night.

Right Now

I love the way mist fills the Common now
when warm air meets the winter's hoard of snow.
You're away. To be precise, as I need
to be more often now, you are at 8
West 8th Street. Probably. What do I know
that isn't before my eyes? March thaws; soon
we'll wake together to a diatribe
of crows. Last year's parsley will show itself,
bitter yellow-green by the curled green hose.

Is that the way *I* will learn to toughen,
wintering over whatever frost comes
to us, yet less tender than last season?
Must I survive?—I understand parsley
has no life or dread of loss to unlearn
but I do. And you—will you be here, as
right now, you are not? Though you are somewhere
as I walk doggedly into this fog,
still breathing, as you, too, are still breathing—

Keep Going

It's not only the accumulation of small slights:
your name misspelled on last evening's program;

the party uptown after the ceremonies and readings—
an editor praising C's poems as if you weren't

standing there beside him, craving appreciation
(or you *were* there, dimming, eclipsed);

then D— your loyal old friend, you'd thought—
leaving without goodbye for a midnight dinner,

clearly, you could see, forgetting you'd flown
down together, shared a Yellow Cab

from the Marine Air Terminal, checked in
to your separate funky rooms at the Gramercy;

petty distresses, trivia you're shamed to be
wounded by, the comedy of literary manners—

How to reconcile these insignificant cuts
with the weight—a boulder, really—pressing

on you as you drive (your brain still crackles
normally, well-organized signals steering

the right foot that accelerates or lifts without
thought, from the pedal), Sunday afternoon

on the Mid-Cape Highway to Provincetown:
no, the small slights aren't what's made you,

you feel, overwhelmed, despairing. There's
E's illness, her doctor calling frantically

last week, the latest test results so desperate
that specialist feared her patient was *dead;*

L's depression, months of lassitude, the trap
of his life sprung with no loophole of escape;

an "official" letter your mother just showed you,
her abandoned cottage condemned, a building

inspector demanding she take action. "Take action":
last year, when you'd nailed plywood to her windows,

hauled away the few good sticks of furniture—
even then, the neglected walls were black, mildewed,

the green daybed rich with mold, a hornet's nest
inside the door, the door lock jimmied, broken,

glistering poison ivy crawling across the floor. . . .
It's *action* she can't take, and your inaction,

watching her tough little body falter
and fail—the largeness of spirit, sacrificial

generosity you hoped for in yourself,
ceded—or unborn; and K, sweet

unathletic K, examining a box turtle
in your yard two days ago, K jaunty

in his faded red baseball cap, then—that night—
tossed in the air by a drunken car,

his face in the morgue, you're told,
unmarred, only *surprised* by the quick

skull-shattering moment of his death.
And now, you hardly notice your brain

(which you picture as hardening, sclerotic),
your brain shifting signals, so the car slows

until a passing driver yells a high-speed curse
that someone else might take as challenging,

even menacing. *Take action:* you accelerate,
again, keep going until the Sahara of dunes

on one side, the brilliant icy bay on the other,
say you're nearly here, whatever's pressing on you,

whatever rides with you, might shrink
in the scouring briny air. And like the survivor

on Everest, the photographer, oxygen deprived,
beyond cold, who stared at his teammate's body

"in perplexity," the exposed outstretched hand,
the familiar shoulder and chest, thinking,

without affect, not curiosity or grief,
How could this have happened to Rob?

his own body not having "room for emotion"
as he waited for assistance, a guide to help him

off the mountain to safety, to *life,*
his camera storing the neutral, fatal images—

like that, you can turn off the road, and pull in.

The Beach

They're not here,
the voice in the machine announced;
and then, omniscient voice:
They won't be back, ever.

But this foggy morning,
on a stony beach I'd never visited,
those patches of light—signals
from those who aren't really gone?

And then, when I reached them,
mist. As if nothing had happened.
Driftwood, white pebbles,
sandblasted bits of colored glass.

The dead:

they're not what's washed out
to sea day after day. They're absence—
lime, or ash, about to become motion
or light. But something tells me

(the tide keeps flooding me
with such wishful thoughts)
the dead will find a way—
couldn't *one?*—to signal me again. . . .

—*after Vittorio Sereni*

Low Tide

Tree of heaven,
the ailanthus so graceful
and disparaged. The "garbage tree."
Who notices its stubborn rhythm
in downtown alleys or gritty
abandoned lots? Junk tree,
at home in soot.

(And why
would I think of it
this minute, walking head down
on the flats, the peculiar hermit crabs
scrabbling away from me, manifest
hysteria in the pearly August
day?)

Undesirable now,
but once carried—precious
cargo—from China for ornament,
for shade. For its tropical attitude.
Ailanthus altissima. Last choice
anywhere other trees grow.
Limbs easily broken;

poisonous roots
invaders of drains
and wells; awful-smelling male
flowers. Allergies. Hay
fever. Disparaged,
undesirable
but still,

graceful,
if you'd look at them
with any sympathy, or hope of pleasure.
Here to stay. Here
to stay.

See how
these little crabs
haul their appropriated
snaily shells into a
blue voracious
bay

To Begin This Way Every Day

at my desk, as my friend John recommends,
   natural as, say, laughing, is for him—
      his whole household still asleep,

his elderly black cat curled
   in dawn's warm oblong of sun,
      Harry's left hand dreaming toward

his somnolent floored guitar,
   Maria's morning visions wayward as lines
      of the story she's been conjuring

for a year in her room with its vista
   of bramble, scrub oak and dunes;
      her garden flailing, the last skeletal

spidery cleomes, the splashy crimson
   dahlias lashed to their green stakes
      against the Cape's September storms.

To begin this way, to take memories
   that strum me before I wake—birth cries,
      circus elephants, Chinese rocks—that lurk

and toss in my windy aching brain,
   then fall, their familiar names set
      somehow wrong, testing me to get them

right, to make sense or song of slant
    arrangements—could I begin there now,
        weightlessly, without deliberation?

When John wasn't writing poems, he said,
    I miss the quirky way my mind works, or
        was it *the way my mind quirks?*—

This drizzly morning, I like to picture him
    at his desk in Truro, to begin to think how
        fortunate we might seem, like gamblers,

browsing and tapping the muddled alphabet
    of keys, door closed hard on the heavy day's
        commands, nerve, or nothing that nameable,

steering our hands; maybe for only one hour,
    this hour, risking what we won yesterday;
        alone, autonomous, capricious, free.

Three Provincetown Mornings

When I lift the window shade
the first blue heron, feeding alone,
stationed in the shallows.

He's early—he must be—great bird
of winter. This last week of August,
his pale face means beautiful bad news.

All summer I meant to write differently,
to find a vocabulary for the harbor,
its excitable transient birds, the dunes

where, twelve years from his death,
Thoreau wrote, *It is wisest to live
without any definite and recognized object*

day to day. Reading that late last night,
I thought, Who'd equal him for laziness?
But I knew it wasn't laziness

when I pictured him on the outer shore,
bent to his notebook, transfigured
by the cold Cape sun, each day

equal to him in interest, in variation.

*

Uninhibited, unedited, the bay
does its green job,
pale and calm as celadon.

Thousands of green species teem—
invisible pastures of plankton,
infinite food factory.

Must *everything* have a purpose?
Even the cool sand sifting
through my morning fingers?

And these hands, is there a task
they're fit for, one that matters?
My own grabbling for *gravitas*

as unapparent to the world as
oceanic life seems—
abstract, indecipherable

viewed like this from the shore.

*

Who'd argue with me if I said
the tide speaks in the voice of Horace:

*The years as they pass plunder us
of one thing then another. . . .*

I would. This tide tells me nothing—
or rather, barefoot in the sand,

I propose a voice tide never needed
as it brings in sea glass, seaworms,

"gray water" from Canadian cruise ships,
then goes back for more. People

like me, facing the bay's glistening
severity, want incident: swimmers,

silvery minnows, sailing ketches. Want
to hear an aphorism, a wave of wisdom.

Here's half a man's shoe, wet and barnacled—
I press it to my ear as if I'm listening.

Insomnia at Daybreak

So many years, so many months and seasons
re-lived in the turnings of one night:
a night of pacing, every comfortless hour
punctuated by the bells of Town Hall.
And now, why should the slow light
of morning hurt so? Like the face
of God, overwhelming, blinding—
hard, effacing face I've taken
for a mirror as the world wakes
yet again.
      Give me the words I need,
the words that would calm my soul,
words that would make my life work.

               —after Vittorio Sereni